KU-021-670

FAIRYTALE DOUGHCRAFT

Anne Skødt

DAVID PORTEOUS
CHUDLEIGH · DEVON

A CIP catalogue record for this book is available from the British Library

ISBN 1 870586 24 7

Published by David Porteous
PO Box 5
Chudleigh
Newton Abbot
Devon TQ13 0YZ

Copyright (c) 1993 Forlaget Klematis
Danish edition copyright (c) 1993 Forlaget Klematis: Eventyrlig Trylledej
English edition copyright (c) 1994 David Porteous

All rights reserved.
No part of this publication may be reproduced, stored in a retrieval system, or transmitted, in any form or by any means, electronic, mechanical, photocopying, recording or otherwise, without prior permission from the publisher.

Translated by Tim Bowler
Typeset by Blanc Verso
Printed and bound in Great Britain
by BPCC Paulton Books Limited

CONTENTS

INTRODUCTION

The inspiration for the figures in this book comes from, among others, the well-known and well-loved fairytales of Hans Christian Andersen and the Brothers Grimm. Although some of the figures are not drawn directly from fairytales, they nevertheless exist very happily in the world of make-believe – clowns, pirates, trolls and witches, for example.

When I was choosing the figures to make, I tried to select those that would appeal particularly to children, for it can be great fun for the whole family to gather in the kitchen and to make figures and shapes from dough. Many of the models on the pages that follow can be made by children aged between six and seven years old, so every one can share in the pleasure. The materials needed to make these dough figures are all relatively inexpensive, so you can make as many as you wish.

Before you begin to make any of the models, read the introductory sections first. Not only do these describe the materials and equipment you will need, they also explain the basic principles that you need to understand before you can really get to grips with making the figures.

The actual recipe for the dough is on page 9. I developed this recipe after a great deal of trial and error, so I hope you enjoy using it. The most important thing is to mix it in the right way; if you do not, the dough may crack and split during the baking.

All the figures are illustrated in full colour. The number in square brackets after the title of the project indicates the page on which the colour illustration will be found. These colour plates can be used as a guide to decorating the figures, but I hope that you will want to experiment with your own favourite colours and patterns. I hope, too, that these models and figures will inspire you to make figures based on your own favourite nursery-rhymes and fairytales.

Have fun.

Anne Skødt

Anne Skødt

TOOLS AND MATERIALS

Make sure that you have the right tools and materials close to hand before you start work. You will probably already have most of the items listed here in your home, but anything you do not already have should be available from your local craft shop.

Ballpoint pen A retractable pen is the easiest way to mark buttons, and it can also be used to mark finger- and toe-nails.

Egg carton Individual egg holders are used as stiffeners in several models.

Fur Use small pieces of fur for hair.

Garlic press This is essential, especially for making hair.

Glue gun This will be useful for all sorts of things. Take care, though, because the glue is warm when it first comes out.

Hole punch The plier-type hole punch can be used to make holes in, say, the king's crown.

Impact adhesive Small parts can be glued to the figures with impact adhesive. The salt in the dough means that some types of glue will not adhere properly.

Lace Use short pieces of lace for decoration and also for marking fine patterns.

Magnet Attach small magnets to the backs of little figures to make perfect figures to attach notes to your refrigerator.

Matchstick or toothpick A thin, pointed stick is useful for marking fingers and ears. You can also use matchsticks or toothpicks as stiffeners inside the figures.

Modelling tools Use a selection of these for moulding, marking and smoothing figures.

Night-light containers Crowns for kings and queens can be simply made from these little containers.

Pastry wheel This useful little tool is perfect for marking patterns – to look like knit wear, for example.

Plant sticks Brooms and sticks can be made from thin sticks.

Ribbon Satin ribbon can be used to hang and decorate the figures.

Rolling pin or bottle Dough does not stick to a marble rolling pin or a glass bottle.

Scissors You will need some scissors to cut the dough. Small, pointed ones – embroidery scissors, perhaps – are best.

Soy Use this in water to give the models a golden surface; see page 16.

Straw A drinking straw can be used to make holes in the dough and to mark patterns.

Varnish when you have decorated the figures, you need to give them a coat of varnish.

Vegetable knife Use a sharp, pointed knife for cutting and marking.

Wire Different gauges of steel wire are used for hanging, spectacles and so on.

Wooden beads A selection of different sizes and colours are ideal decorations.

MAGIC DOUGH

For best results you must use the right recipe and mix it correctly. You can vary the proportions of the ingredients slightly depending on how dry or moist the room is. If the dough becomes too dry, add more water. If it becomes too moist, add more flour. If you want to make larger quantities, use a mixer to make the dough.

Dough that is to be used by children should, ideally, be rather dry because children usually take longer to model and mould the dough, which picks up moisture from their hands as they work.

Recipe

5 cups "expensive" flour
3 cups "cheap" flour
3 cups fine salt
3 cups of warm water
2 tablespoons cooking oil

Mix the flours and salt together, then mix in the water and oil, blended together. Knead the dough for 5–10 minutes, until it is smooth and pliable.

Test to see if the dough is the right consistency by rolling out an oblong sausage and holding the sausage between two fingers. If it gets longer, the dough is too soft and you should knead in more flour. If it keeps its shape, the consistency is right.

It's important to use two grades of flour. If you use only the cheap flour, the dough will be too heavy to work with and is likely to crack during baking. If you use only the better quality, expensive flour, the dough will be too light and will not keep its shape.

The oil makes the dough malleable and easy to handle, and it also helps to prevent cracks forming during the baking process.

When the dough has been thoroughly kneaded, leave it to rest for 1–2 hours before you use it. Wrap the dough in a plastic bag and leave it to stand in a cool place. Do not put it in the refrigerator, though, because that is too cold.

While you are modelling a figure, leave the portion of dough you are not using wrapped up tightly in the plastic bag so that it does not dry out and become difficult to work with.

MODELLING

Before you begin, lay some grease-proof paper on your work surface. This makes it easier to move the figure when, say, you need to move it to the baking tray.

The separate parts of the model should be "glued" together with water, and it is easiest to use your fingers to apply the water. You will also need water to smooth the model. You must wash your hands frequently while you work. Not only will you wash off any dough or salt, which might mark and spoil your model, but if you allow salt to build up on your hands it could cause a skin irritation.

You should also keep your work surface clean, so that small pieces of discarded dough do not adhere to and mark your models.

When you have finished modelling the figure or figures, make a small hanging loop from wire.

Spherical Figures [15]

These figures are fairly easy to make and are, therefore, good to start with. They are sufficiently easy for children of six or seven years old to try.

1 Roll a ball for the body and press the neck into shape so that the dough is pear-shaped (Fig. 1).
2 Use a vegetable knife to cut the legs (Fig. 2). If you are making a girl, do not separate the legs, but mould the bottom part of the ball into a dress.
3 Roll two small balls for the feet and attach them to the bottom of the legs (Fig. 3).
4 Roll a sausage for the arms and cut it in half at an angle (Fig. 4). Attach the arms at either side of the body (Fig. 5).
5 Roll two small balls and attach them to the ends of the arms. Roll a larger ball for the head and a small ball for the nose (Fig. 6). If you want, roll two small balls for the ears.
6 Mark the ears and nose with a ball-point pen.
7 Make the hair by pushing some dough through a garlic press (Fig. 7).
8 Finish off by making a hanging loop from strong wire and pushing the long ends well down inside the figure, pressing the dough gently together around the wire (Fig. 8).

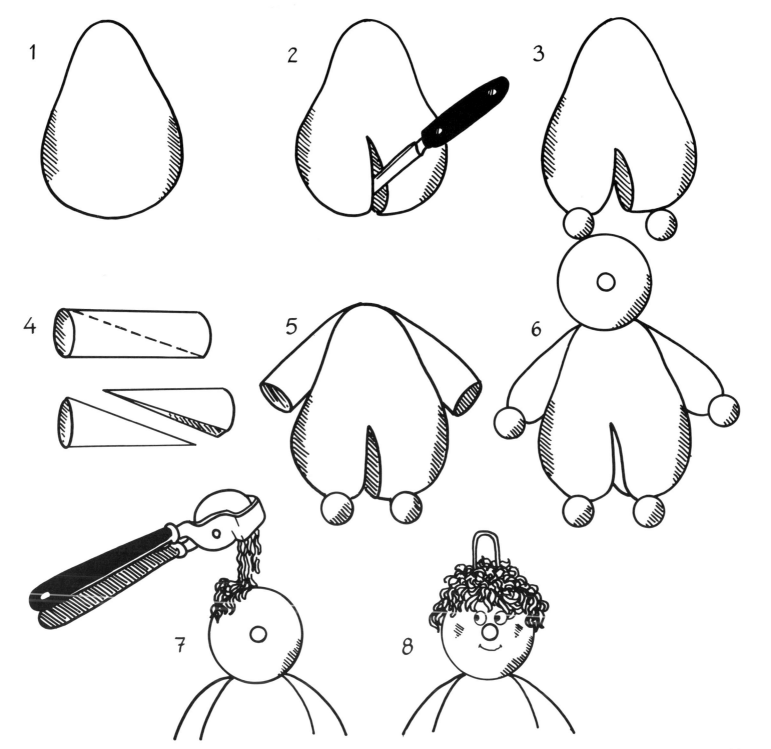

Sausage Figures [15]

These figures are more complicated than the spherical figures because they have more separate parts, but once you are used to working with the dough you will find them quite easy to model. We will make two figures to start with: first a boy with short trousers and, on page 14, a girl in a dress.

Boy

1 Roll a sausage for the legs, divide it and place the two pieces side by side (Fig. 1).

2 Roll a short, thick sausage and place it above the two long sausages to give the figure its thickness. Do not press it too flat (Fig. 2).

3 Roll a sheet of dough to 3–4mm (about ⅛in) thick and cut the pieces for the shirt, trousers and pockets (Fig. 3).

4 Place the shirt on the body so that the top edge is against the top of the legs. Press the shirt gently in at the sides (Fig. 4).

5 Place the trouser section over the legs and press it gently in at the sides. Cut the section between the legs and press the piece lightly down around the legs (Fig. 5).

6 Roll a sausage for the arms and cut it at an angle. Attach the arms to the body (Fig. 6).

7 Attach the pockets to the trousers. If you want, make the boy have a hand in one of the pockets by cutting the arm at an angle. It is easier to do this before you attach the arms.

8 Push a matchstick down through the top of the body as a stiffener (Fig. 7).

9 Roll small balls for the hands and attach them to the arms, unless the hands are in the pockets, and use a modelling tool to mark the fingers.

10 Press the feet into shape with a modelling tool or roll small balls.

11 Roll a ball for the head and press it down on top of the matchstick.

12 Roll small balls for the nose and ears, and mark them when you have positioned them on the head.

13 Make some hair with a garlic press, then attach a hanging loop (Fig. 8).

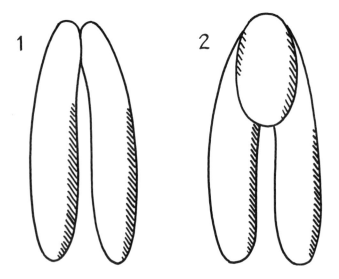

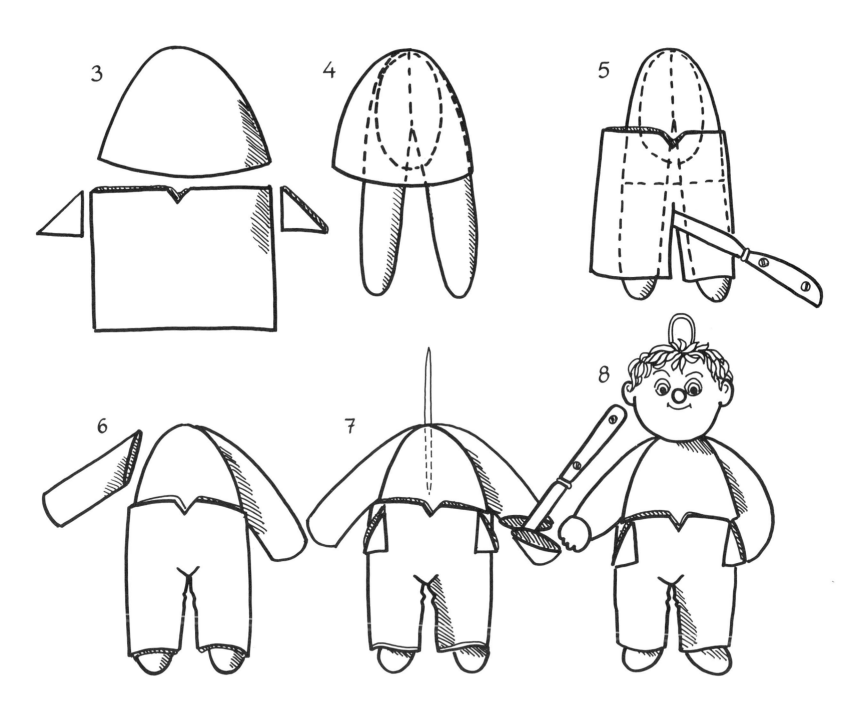

Girl

1 Form the legs and body as in steps 1 and 2 on page 12.

2 Shape the body by rolling two balls, about the size of hazel nuts and attach them to the top of the body (Fig. 1).

3 Roll out a piece of dough to 3–4mm (about 1/8in) thick and cut a dress (Fig. 2).

4 Place the dress loosely on the body so that the top edge lines up with top of the body. Try to place the dough so that the dress falls into smooth folds. Use a modelling tool to help create the shape of the folds from underneath (Fig. 3).

5 Roll a sausage for the arms, cut it at an angle and attach the arms to the body.

6 Roll small balls for hands and attach them to the arms. Use a modelling tool to mark the fingers.

7 Shape the feet with a modelling tool or roll small balls.

8 Make the head, nose, ears and hair and attach a hanging loop as described in steps 11–13 on page 12.

When you start to make the models shown in this book you will find that you can easily adapt and make your own variations of the basic shapes. For example, you can give boy figures long or short trousers or you could add a bow tie. Girl figures often have hats. Many of the figures wear jackets or coats, and when you make these you should always join on the arms after the jacket of coat. When the models have special costumes – the clown on page 21 and Harlequin on page 29, for example – the figures are described individually.

When the instructions tell you to cut out the separate parts from a sheet of dough, you should assume that a sheet 3–4mm (about 1/8in) thick is meant. If the dough needs to be thicker or thinner, this will be stated in the text.

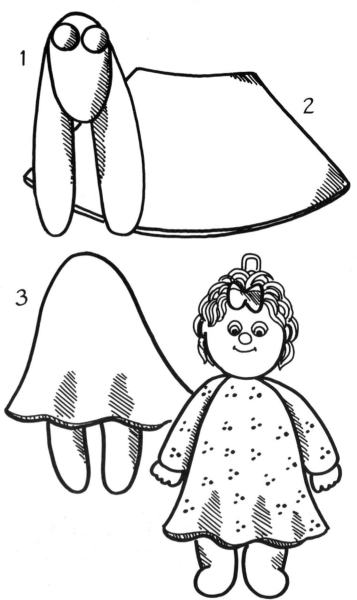

Modelling the basic figures (see pages 10–14).

BAKING AND DECORATING

One of the great advantages of dough is that you do not need a special oven or kiln as you do with, say, clay or pottery. You can use your normal kitchen oven. For best results and to avoid cracks forming in the dough it is important to put the figures in the oven as soon as you have finished working on them. If you are making several figures and want to bake them together, cover the baking tray with plastic film to stop the completed figures from drying out.

Bake larger figures for 3–4 hours at about 150°C (300°F/gas mark 2), although the length of time will, of course, depend on how thick the figures are. Small or flat models should be baked for about 2 hours at approximately 100°C (225°F/gas mark ¼). These times and temperatures are only approximate and will vary according to your oven type, so you will need to experiment. However, you should always aim to bake just one tray at a time, which should be placed in the centre of the oven.

You can give the head, hair, hands and legs an attractive golden colour by brushing them with a mixture of 2 parts soy to 3 parts water just after you take the figures out of the oven – that is, while they are still warm. If you want a figure to have white hair, do not paint it. The colour illustration on page 57 shows the difference between the ladies-in-waiting, whose hair was not coloured with soy, and the swineherd, whose hair was coloured. It might be a good idea to experiment with the soy mixture on an area that is going to be painted later so that you can assess the colour.

Decorating the models is the most exciting aspect of making dough figures, and if you use the right tools and materials and are prepared to

go to a little trouble, you will achieve some stunning results. Make sure the figures are absolutely dry before you begin to decorate.

Begin by applying a coat of varnish. Take care to cover the whole surface, front and back, so that no moisture can penetrate. The varnish also provides a better base for many of the paints that you will use. Some craft shops stock oil-based varnishes that are specially formulated for dough. Do not use a water-based varnish, or the water will combine with the dough. When you apply paints and varnishes, always work in a well-ventilated room and make sure that children do not use any of the oil-based preparations. Leave the varnish to dry for 6–8 hours.

You can then begin to paint the figures, and now you can let the children help. All the models in this book have been decorated with acrylic paint, which is a water-based hobby paint that is non-toxic and odourless. It contains no solvent, and brushes can be washed in water. This kind of paint dries in about 15 minutes, which is an additional advantage when you want to decorate plain surfaces.

Craft shops also stock some special felt-tipped pens, which contain concentrated colour that can be applied in almost the same way as paints, and many people find the pens easier to use than paintbrushes.

Painting Clothes and Accessories

Do not paint the face, hands and legs or your figures nor, in most cases, the hair.

Larger surfaces should be painted twice so that you can be certain that the paint covers completely. You will need at least three brushes – numbers 000, 0 and 4. Number 4, which is the largest, is used for large areas. Number 0 is used for small figures and for reaching into difficult corners. Brush number 000 is the finest brush, and you should use it to paint facial features and patterns and stripes on clothes and accessories.

Painting Faces

The face is usually the most important part of the figure because it imparts the character and personality. It is, therefore, worth taking extra care over it and using the right brushes and paints. Use a number 000 for all the details.

1 Begin by painting the eyes white. Leave the paint to dry.

2 Paint a mid-blue circle in the white.

3 Add a black pupil in the centre of each eye.

4 Paint the outline of the girl's eyes with black, then add the eyelashes and eyebrows.

5 On the boy, mark only the top part of the eye shape, then add the eyebrows.

6 Paint the girl's mouth red and the boy's mouth brown.

SMALL FIGURES [19]

These small figures are easy to make and you can combine elements from the different figures as you please. Begin by making the basic figure as described on pages 10–11.

Troll

1 Roll thin sausages for the tail, braces and belt and attach them.
2 Cut out the mouth with a knife and add two small teeth.
3 Glue some hair, made from fur, to the head and to the end of the tail.

Clown

1 Roll a thin sausage for the belt, gently press it flat and put it in place.
2 Cut two jacket sections from a thin sheet of dough and put them in place before attaching the arms. Make and attach a button and bow tie.
3 Mould the hat out of two balls. Press one of the flat to act as a brim, and place the other on top.

Pirate

1 Roll two thin sausages to make the belt. Twist them together and put them in position.
2 Mould a bottle and place it in one of the hands.
3 Cut the scarf, eye patch and kerchief for the head from a sheet of dough and attach them.
4 Use a modelling tool to make the scars on the cheek and stomach.
5 Make a small ring from a piece of wire and press it into the nose.

Fridge Magnets

Bake these small figures at 100°C (225°F/gas mark ¼). When the figures have been baked, glue small magnets to the backs so that you can use them to hold notes and lists to the metal door of the fridge.

1 Make the basic figure of the bear as shown on pages 10–11. Mould the ears, nose and tummy from balls.
2 Make the figure of the troll as shown on pages 10–11 and on page 18.
3 The gingerbread house is described on pages 46–7. The house is covered in little balls that have been pressed flat.
4 Roll a ball for the head of the clown and make the hat. Decorate the hat with small balls and cut the bow tie from a thin sheet of dough.

Nameplates

Use these nameplates on bedroom doors or as table cards at a children's party. Because they are small, bake them at 100°C (225°F/gas mark ¼), and if the sheets of dough start to bulge, prick them with a needle to allow the air to escape. Use a sheet of dough rolled to about 10mm (less than ½in) thick, and make a hole in the top of each one with a straw or attach a loop made of wire.

1 Use a small glass to press out the round plate for the girl.
2 Cut out the mattress and bed for the princess and the pea with a pastry wheel, which can also be used to mark the joins between the mattresses. Don't forget the ball for the pea.
3 Use a knife to cut out the plate for the clown.
4 The troll's plate was cut with pastry wheel.

Small figures, fridge magnets and nameplates (see page 18).

CLOWNS [23]

Clown with a Cap

This colourful character, with his red jacket and orange hair, is carrying an accordion in one hand.

1 Make the basic figure as shown on pages 12–13, but give the figure long trousers.
2 Decorate the shirt with a modelling tool and use the end of a ballpoint pen to indicate the buttons.
3 Cut two jacket pieces from a sheet of dough and put the sections in place.
4 Bend the top part of the jacket back and cut a triangle out of each side to make the revers.
5 Cut two pockets, and fold down the top of each and place them on the jacket. Make a button from a ball of dough, press it flat and position it on the jacket.

6 Fold a strip of dough in a zigzag and make the end pieces of the accordion from small pieces of dough, slightly larger than the accordion itself. Make small loops from wire and attach one end of the accordion to one of the clown's hands.
7 Cut a bow tie from a sheet of dough and put it in place.
8 Mould the cap from two balls of dough. Press one flat to make the brim and place the other on top as the crown. Fold the brim back at the front and place it on the head.
8 After baking and decorating the clown, tie small bows of embroidery cotton and glue them to the shoes.

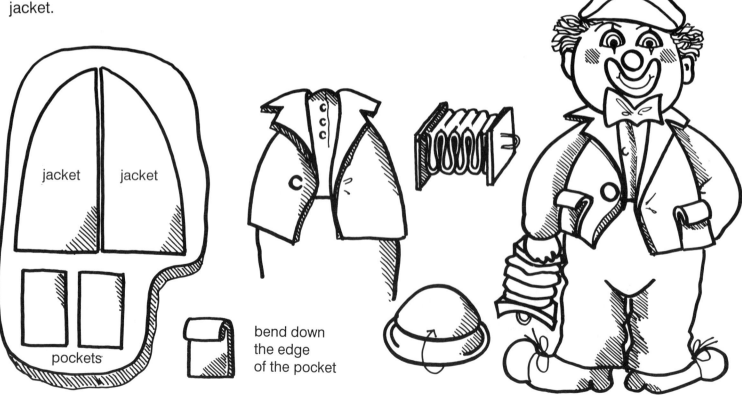

jacket jacket

pockets

bend down the edge of the pocket

Juggling Clown

The balls are wooden beads, threaded onto a piece of wire and glued in place.

1 Make the basic figure as shown on pages 12–13 but do not add a shirt or trousers.

2 Cut the costume from a sheet of dough and place it on the body. Cut the costume between the legs as shown in the illustration.

3 Cut narrow strips for the frills around the cuffs and ankles. Fold them in a zigzag and put them in place.

4 Cut a wider strip for the collar, fold it and place it around the neck.

5 Mould a hat from a ball of dough and model it as shown below so that it fits the head.

6 Roll balls of dough and place them on the hat and the front of the costume. Prick them with a toothpick to make them look like woollen pompons.

7 Thread the beads on a piece of wire and attach the wire to the clown's hands as shown in the illustration.

8 After baking and decorating the clown, tie small bows of embroidery cotton and glue them to the shoes.

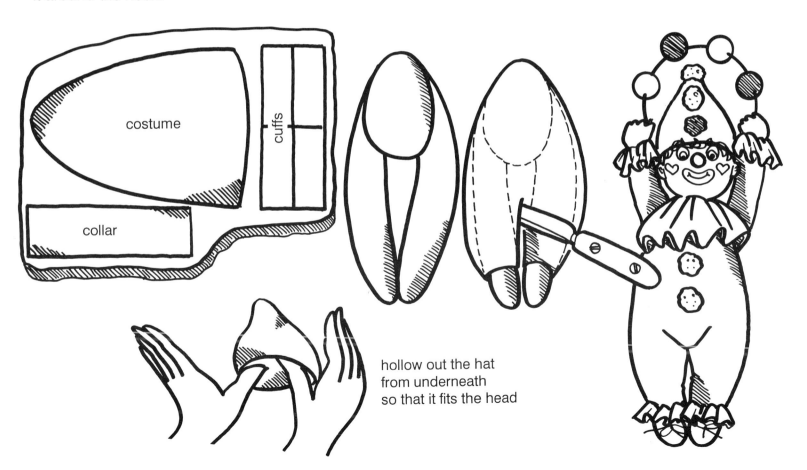

costume

cuffs

collar

hollow out the hat
from underneath
so that it fits the head

White-faced Clown

This is the most elegant of the clowns and, as is tradition, his face should be painted white.

1 Make the basic figure as shown on pages 12–13 but do not put any tousers on it.

2 Use a modelling tool to decorate the shirt and use a ballpoint pen for the buttons.

3 Cut narrow strips for the lace on the shirt, fold them in a zigzag and place them on the front of the shirt.

4 Cut two pieces for the costume from a sheet of dough, place them on the body and press them gently together, making an indentation around the stomach and pressing the pieces together between the legs. Use a modelling tool to press the waist into shape.

5 Bend the top of the costume sections backwards to form revers.

6 Press two small balls flat to make buttons for the costume.

7 Model a musical instrument and place it in one of the hands.

8 Roll two little sausages and position them as the tops of the clown's socks. Make two buckles for the shoes.

9 Cut a bow tie from a sheet of dough.

10 Mould the hat as described on page 21 and place it on the head.

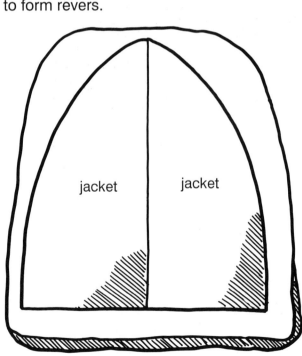

jacket   jacket

bend the
top sections
of the jacket
backwards

Clown with a cap (see page 20); juggling clown (see page 21); white-faced clown (see page 22).

PIRATES [27]
Pirate Captain

The captain has lost one of his legs in a battle on the high seas. Don't forget his parrot.

1 Make the basic figure as shown on pages 12–13 but cut off one leg at the knee. Fit the trousers inside the shirt.
2 Use a modelling tool to mark folds on the trousers and indicate the buttons with a ballpoint pen.
3 Stick a thin leg into the short leg.
4 Cut two waistcoat sections from a sheet of dough and put them in place.
5 Cut a strip for the cross-belt and place it over the waistcoat. Make a buckle from a small roll.
6 Mould a sheath and a revolver stock and fit the parts into the belt.
7 Cut a strip for a lace ruff, fold it in a zigzag and put it in place around the neck.

8 Cut two jacket sections from a sheet of dough and arrange them so that they fall in folds.
9 Bend the jacket pieces backwards at the neck and at the bottom of the hem.
10 Cut pockets (see page 20).
11 Press small balls flat to make buttons for the jacket front and the pockets.
12 Put a thick stick under one of the arms as a crutch, moulding a sausage to go at the top of the crutch and around the arm.
13 Cut strips for the frilled cuffs, ruffle them and fit them to the sleeves above the hands.
14 Mould a parrot as shown in the colour illustration and put it on the pirate's shoulder.
15 Use a garlic press to make a beard and fix it on the head. Add the eye patch.
16 Cut the hat from a sheet of dough, which should be about 10mm (less then ½in) thick, and place it at the front of the head with a piece of dough behind it to pad it (see illustration below).

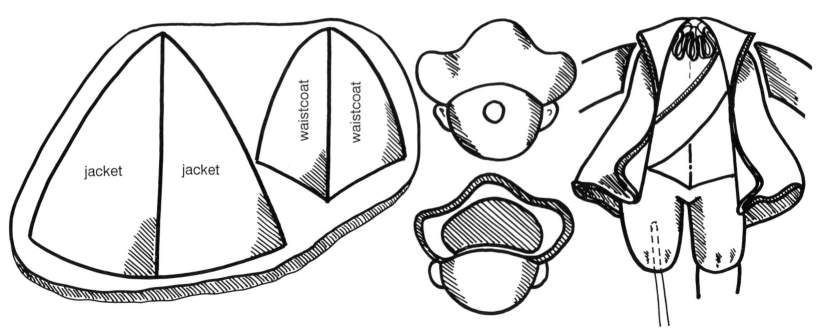

Pirate King

The pirate king loves to go sailing off on adventures with his good friend the pirate captain.

1 Make the basic figure as shown on pages 12–13 and fit the trousers inside the shirt.

2 Use a modelling tool to decorate the shirt and use a ballpoint pen to indicate the buttons down the front.

3 Cut narrow strips for the lace down the front of the shirt, folding them zigzag fashion.

4 Cut two wide strips for the belt. Decorate them with a pastry wheel, place them around the waist and tie them together.

5 Cut two waistcoat sections and two sleeves from a sheet of dough and position the waistcoat pieces.

6 Attach the arms and fit the short sleeves around the top of the arms, ruffling the edges of the sleeves to ease the fit around the shoulders.

7 Make handles for the knife and sword and attach them to the hands.

8 Cut the blades for the knife and sword from kitchen foil.

9 Model the shoes so that they turn up at the toes and attach them to the legs.

10 Use a garlic press to make the beard and position it on the face.

11 Mould the hat from a ball and hollow it out so that it fits on the head. Use a modelling tool to mark the creases in the hat.

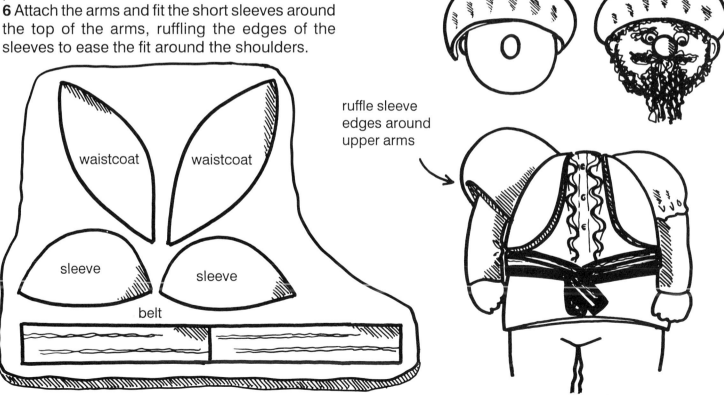

waistcoat   waistcoat

sleeve   sleeve

belt

ruffle sleeve edges around upper arms

Cabin Boy

The cabin boy has climbed up in the rigging to keep look-out. He hangs on with one hand and waves the jolly roger in the other.

1 Make the basic figure as shown on pages 12–13. Instead of a small, short sausage, use a large ball for the stomach, and when you put on the shirt, make sure that it is too short so that the boy's stomach is visible. Use a matchstick to mark the navel and make the bottom edge of the shirt a little frayed.

2 Cut the flag and kerchief for the boy's head from a sheet of dough.

3 Use a matchstick for the flagstaff and bend one hand around it.

4 Place the kerchief around the head.

5 Make some hair and fold it up around the edge of the kerchief.

6 Position one arm so that it points upwards and bend the hand around a stick.

7 Make an earring from a small piece of wire.

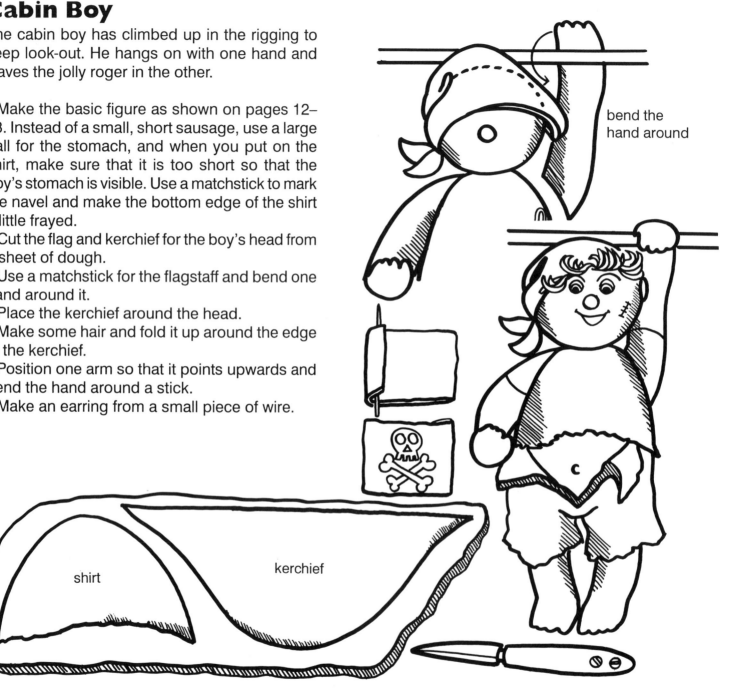

bend the hand around

shirt

kerchief

Pirate captain (see page 24); pirate king (see page 25); cabin boy (see page 26).

PIERROT, HARLEQUIN AND COLUMBINE [31]

These figures are characters from traditional pantomime. Harlequin frustrates all the tricks of the clown, who is in love with Columbine.

Pierrot

1 Make the basic figure as shown on pages 12–13, making the trousers long.

2 Cut a section for the jacket from a sheet of dough and put it in place around the body.

3 Roll three balls for buttons and fit them on the jacket. Prick the balls with a toothpick to make them look like woollen pompons.

4 Use a small cup or glass to press the hat out of a sheet of dough and mould it as shown .

press the hat carefully into shape at the sides after you have placed it on the head

hat

jacket

28

Harlequin

1 Make the basic figure as shown on pages 12–13 but do not add a shirt or trousers.

2 Make the costume, but with short legs, as described on page 21 and put it in place.

3 Cut a narrow strip for a belt and put it around the waist. Roll a small sausage for the buckle.

4 Cut three small strips and make them into ruffles to make a jabot at the neck.

5 Cut a mask and hat from a sheet of dough and fit them to the figure.

ruffle narrow strips of dough and place them at Harlequin's neck

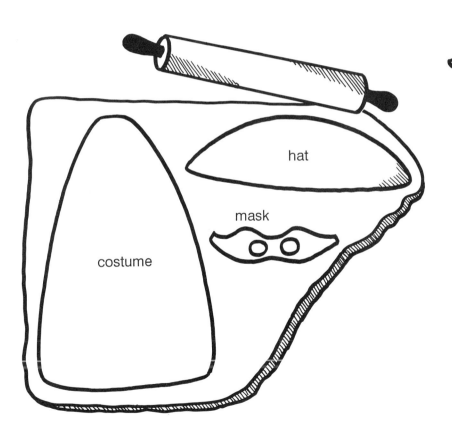

hat

mask

costume

Columbine

1 Make the basic figure as shown on page 14, placing one leg so that it turns out to the side.

2 Cut a full dress from a sheet of dough and place it over the body, arranging the folds carefully.

3 Cut two collar sections from a sheet of dough and arrange them over the shoulders.

4 Mould a small rose as shown in the illustration and attach it to Columbine's hair.

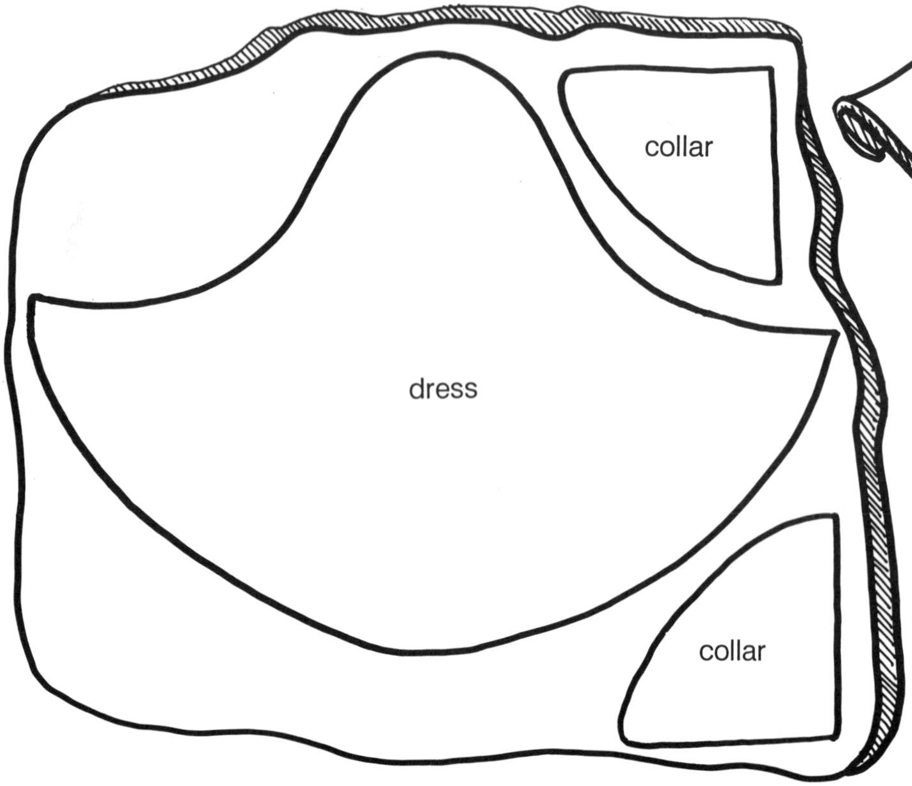

collar

dress

collar

make a rose from small, flat pieces of dough

Pierrot (see page 28); Harlequin (see page 29); Columbine (see page 30).

CHARLIE CHAPLIN [35]

Charlie Chaplin, the king of silent comedy, is not difficult to make, and the decoration is simple, too, because he is dressed in black and white.

1 Make the basic figure as shown on pages 12–13, making the trousers long.
2 Use a modelling tool to decorate the shirt and use a ballpoint pen to indicate the buttons.
3 Cut narrow strips for the braces and front of the trousers and position them as shown.
4 Make the jacket as described on page 20.
5 Cut triangular pockets as shown on pages 12–13 and put them in place.
6 Press two small balls flat and position them as buttons on the jacket.
7 Cut a bow tie from a sheet of dough and put it in position.
8 Mould the hat from two balls of dough. Press one ball flat to form the brim and put the other on top as the crown. Place the hat on the head.
9 Use a garlic press to make strands for the hair, eyebrows and moustache.
10 Push a thin stick into one hand so that it looks like a walking-stick.
11 When you have baked and decorated the figure, tie small bows of embroidery cotton and glue them to the shoes.

cut narrow strips for the braces and front of the trousers

pockets

mould the hat from two balls of dough, pressing one flat for the brim with the other on top for the crown

STRONG MAN [35]

The strong man appears at the circus and performs amazing tricks. The dumbbell is made from large wooden beads, which are attached to a wooden stick and painted once the figure has been baked.

1 Roll a large ball for the body and press it into shape. Mark the navel with a matchstick.
2 Roll sausages for the legs and attach the legs to the body.
3 Make short trousers as shown on pages 12–13 and turn over the top of the trousers.
4 Mark the toes with a modelling tool.
5 Roll a ball for the head and attach it as shown on pages 12–13.
6 Roll sausages for the arms and put them in position, marking the fingers with a modelling tool.
7 Bend the hands around a wooden stick (attach and paint the beads once the figure has been baked).
8 Make hair, the moustache and chest hair with a garlic press and put it in place.

bend the hands around the stick

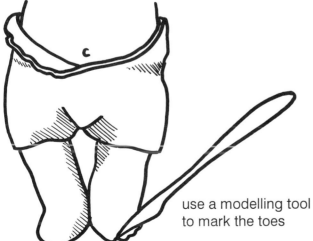

use a modelling tool to mark the toes

33

MAGICIAN [35]

1 Make the basic figures as shown on pages 12—13, but make the trousers long.

2 Use a modelling tool to decorate the shirt and use a ballpoint pen to indicate the buttons.

3 Cut a side strip from a sheet of dough for the cummerbund and decorate it with a pastry wheel.

4 Cut two waistcoat sections from a sheet of dough and put them in place.

5 Cut two jacket pieces and two tail pieces from a sheet of dough.

6 Put the jacket pieces in place and bend back the front to form revers.

7 Attach the coat tails under the arms, shaping the tails so that they are slightly rounded.

8 Make a rabbit as shown below and attach it to one hand.

9 Make the magician's hat from two balls and attach it to the other hand.

10 Cut a bow tie from a sheet of dough and put it in place under the chin.

11 Make a moustache and hair with a garlic press.

waistcoat

waistcoat

jacket

tail

jacket

tail

make the magician's hat from two balls of dough

34

Charlie Chaplin (see page 32); strong man (see page 33); magician (see page 34).

TROLLS [39]

In Icelandic mythology, trolls are evil giants, but our trolls are a family of mischievous dwarfs, who live in the hills of Scandinavia and are skilled in all aspects of metal work.

Boy Troll

1 Make the basic figure as shown on pages 12–13, but instead of using a small, short sausage, form the stomach from a large ball. When you make the shirt, it should be short enough to reveal the stomach and navel. Mark the navel with a matchstick.

2 Roll a long sausage for the tail and put it in place.

3 Put a small patch on one trouser knee.

4 After you have baked and decorated the figure, glue hair to the head and to the end of the tail.

mark around the patch with a modelling tool

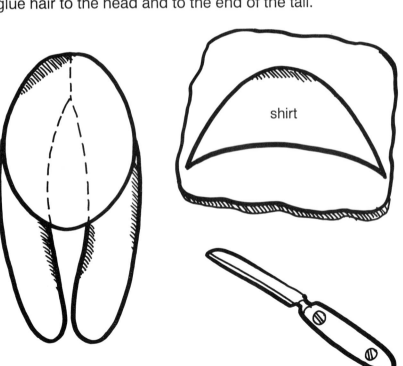

shirt

Girl Troll

1 Make the basic figure as shown on page 14.

2 Cut two sleeve pieces from a sheet of dough and fit them around the arms, making sure that they are open.

3 Make a tail from a thin sausage and put it in place.

4 Make a couple of patches for the dress.

5 When you have baked and decorated the figure, glue some hair to the head and to the end of the tail.

make sure
the sleeves
are open

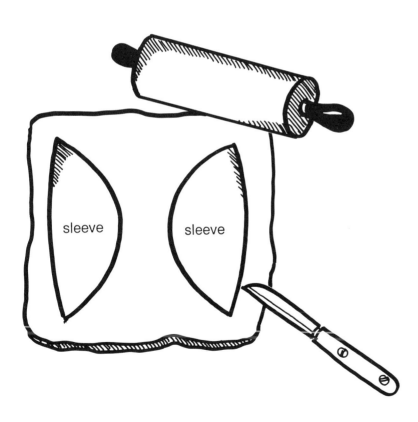

sleeve   sleeve

Teenage Trolls

1 Make the basic figures as shown on pages 12–13. The trousers of one of the trolls should be made to look like dungarees.

2 Mark the shirt opening with a modelling tool and use a ballpoint pen to indicate the buttons.

3 Cut narrow strips for the braces and put them in position.

4 Cut two waistcoat pieces from a sheet of dough and put the pieces in place on one of the figures.

5 Mark a pocket on the waistcoat with a modelling tool and flatten a ball of dough to make a button.

6 If you wish, add a collar by fitting two narrow strips of dough around the neck.

7 Mould a hammer as shown in the colour illustration and give it to one of the trolls to hold.

cut out the mouth with a knife and make a tooth

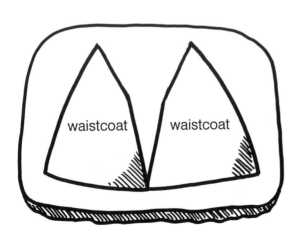

waistcoat   waistcoat

Boy troll (see page 36); girl troll (see page 37); teenage trolls (see page 38).

S. OW WHITE A. D THE SEVE. DWAR S [41]

This is one of everyone's favourite fairy stories. You will find instructions for making the dwarfs on pages 42–3.

Snow White

1 Make a cone shape from a semicircle of card and staple the sides together.
2 Roll a sheet of dough 5–6mm (about ¼in) thick and cut a circular skirt. Lay it over the cone, arranging it to hang in natural-looking folds.
3 Press a thin stick through the centre of the cone so that it protrudes by 2–3cm (about 1in).
4 Cut the front and back sections for the dress out of a sheet of dough 3–4mm (about ⅛in) thick.

5 Roll two sausages for the arms, press them into shape and attach them to the sides of the body.
6 Cut out two sleeves and place them over the arms.
7 Cut out the collar and place it around the neck.
8 Bake the figure for an hour.
9 When the figure has cooled down, roll a ball for the head and press it down over the stick. Roll a small ball for the nose and put it in position.
10 Bake the figure for a further hour.
11 Use a garlic press to make the hair and put it in position before baking the figure for a further hour.

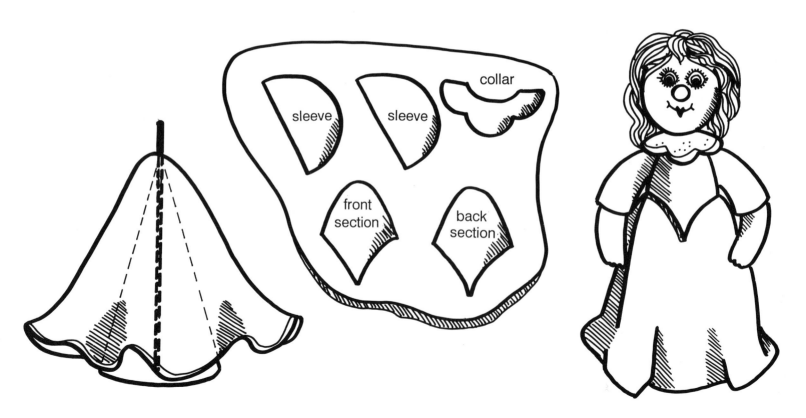

Snow White and the Seven Dwarfs (see pages 40–43).

The Dwarfs

The dwarf described on this page is sitting down. If you wish, you can give him a jacket as shown in the illustration on page 41.

1 Cut a cone from an egg box, roll a sheet of dough and use it to cover the cone.
2 Cut a narrow strip for the belt and put it in position, using a thin sausage to make the buckle.
3 Roll two sausages for the legs and attach them to the cone as shown.
4 Mould two pointed shoes and attach them to the legs.
5 Roll two sausages for the arms and attach them to the sides of the body.
6 Mould two small balls for the hands and attach them to the arms.

7 Press a matchstick through the top of the body as a support for the head.
8 Roll a ball for the head and press it over the matchstick.
9 Roll small balls for the nose and, if you wish, the ears.
10 Use a garlic press to make the hair, eyebrows and beard.
11 When the dwarf is baked and decorated make a cap from the finger of an old pair of knitted gloves.

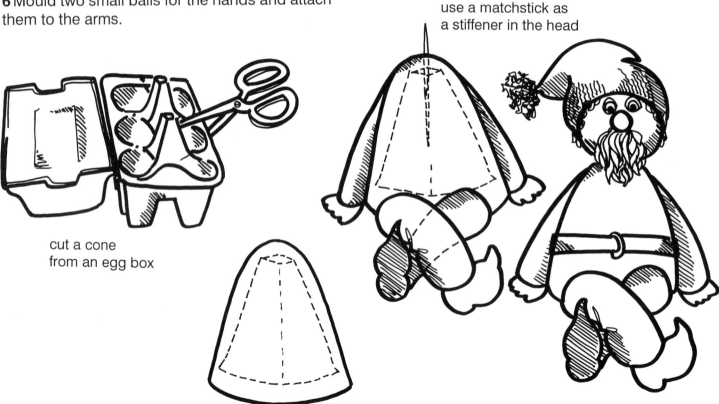

cut a cone
from an egg box

use a matchstick as
a stiffener in the head

The dwarf described here is lying down. Some variations in the basic position are shown in the colour illustration on page 41.

1 Roll two sausages for the legs and lay them side by side.

2 If you wish, bend one leg slightly up and use half a matchstick to stiffen it (see the illustration below).

3 Roll a ball and press it into an oblong shape. Place it over the legs as shown in the illustration.

4 Cut the jacket from a sheet of dough and place it around the body so that it reaches as far as the legs. Press it down a little here.

5 Mould small pointed shoes and attach them to the legs.

6 Mould the head, arms and hands and attach the parts, using a matchstick to strengthen the neck joint.

7 Make hair, moustache, beard and eyebrows with a garlic press and put them in position.

8 When you have baked and painted the dwarf, make a cap from the finger of an old pair of knitted gloves.

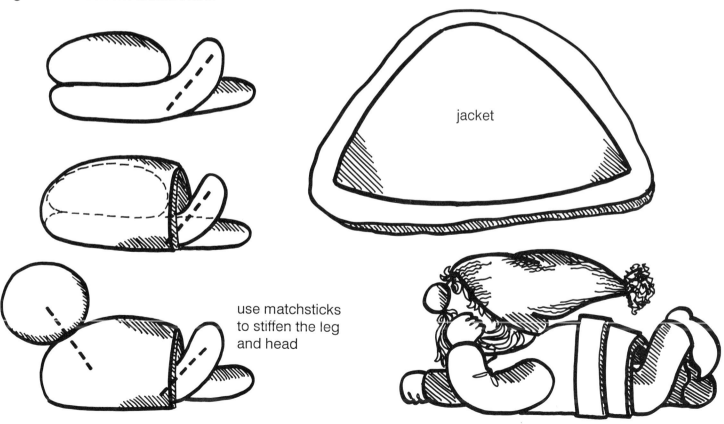

jacket

use matchsticks to stiffen the leg and head

HANSEL AND GRETEL [45]

Instructions for making Hansel and Gretel are given on this page, and the gingerbread house is described on pages 46–7.

1 Make the basic boy and girl figures as explained on pages 12–14. Make Hansel's trousers slightly tattered around the bottom edges.

2 Cut out the pinafore from a sheet of dough and put it in place around Gretel.

3 Cut a narrow strip of dough for the braces of Hansel's trousers and indicate the buttons with a ballpoint pen.

4 Make hair for both figures in a garlic press.

5 Make a biscuit for Hansel to hold and a pretzel for Gretel.

mark buttons with the end of a ballpoint pen

pinafore

Hansel and Gretel and the Gingerbread House (see pages 44–7).

This is the house in which Hansel and Gretel were held captive by the wicked witch. It will look best if you leave most of it uncoloured.

1 Roll a sheet of dough about 15mm (½in) thick and cut out the house. Because the roof should be twice as thick as the base, cut out an extra triangle for the roof and lay it on top (see illustrations below).

2 Use a sharp knife to cut out the door and windows. When you bake the house, replace the door. If you want the door to stand ajar, support it with a small piece of kitchen foil.

3 Cover the whole roof with little circles, pressed from balls of dough, and arrange them like tiles by starting at the bottom and working upwards.

4 Twist some pretzels from little sausages of dough and arrange them along the sides of the house and above the door.

5 Roll two sausages for the sides of the door. You can later paint these to look like sticks of candy.

6 Mould little circles to go around the widow frames. When the house has been baked, paint them brown and, before the paint is dry, sprinkle some granulated sugar or coarse salt over them.

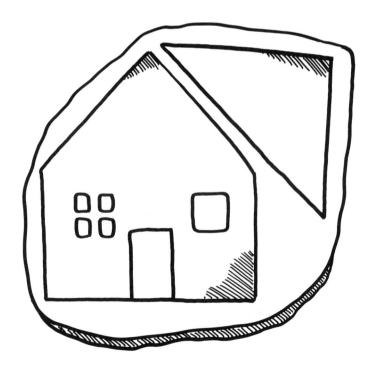

1 Roll a ball for the witch's head.
2 Make a nose from a small sausage and attach it to the head.
3 Make hair with a garlic press and put it in place.
4 Cut a headscarf from a sheet of dough and wrap it around the head.
5 Mould two small hands.
6 Place the witch's head and hands so that she seems to be looking out of one of the windows.

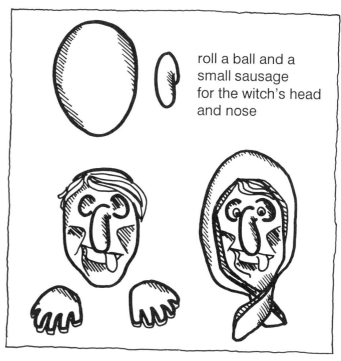

roll a ball and a small sausage for the witch's head and nose

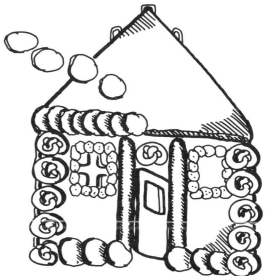

THE PRINCESS AND THE PEA [49]

The princess is lying on all those mattresses, but she still can't get to sleep, and if you look between the two bottom mattresses you will see why.

1 Cut the piece of dough for the mattresses out a sheet of dough and indicate the divisions between them with a ruler, pressing it down gently into the dough and taking care not to go all the way through.

2 Roll a small pea and place it between the two bottom mattresses.

3 Roll two long sausages for bedposts and attach them to either side of the mattresses.

4 Roll two thin sausages and wrap them around the foot of the bedposts.

5 Cut a wide piece of dough for the curtain over the top of the bed, press it into shape, using a modelling tool to mark the creases.

6 Roll two small balls into finials for the tops of the bedposts and press them into position.

7 Mould a pillow and place it near to the left-hand bedpost.

8 Make the head and legs of the princess from a ball and two sausages as shown in the illustration. Shape the feet with a modelling tool.

9 Cut a small quilt from a sheet of dough and lay it over the princess.

10 Roll two sausages for the arms and position them as shown.

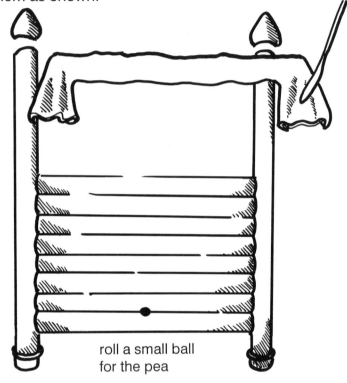

roll a small ball
for the pea

use a ruler to
mark the divisions
between the
mattresses

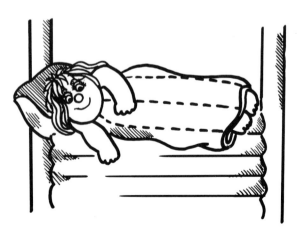

The princess and the pea (see page 48).

LITTLE RED RIDING HOOD [53]

The characters from this famous tale are shown on the following pages. Red Riding Hood herself, with her basket of goodies, is shown below, the Huntsman is described on page 51 and Grandmother is shown on page 52.

Little Red Riding Hood

1 Make the basic figure as shown on page 14.

2 Cut a pinafore from a sheet of dough.

3 Cut two cloak pieces and the bonnet and arrange them in position.

4 Turn up the brim of the bonnet.

5 Make a little basket from strips of dough as shown in the illustration and attach it at the bottom edge of the pinafore. Use a modelling tool to decorate the basket.

6 Make a little bottle from dough and place it in the basket before the figure is baked.

7 When the figure has been baked, ruffle a piece of lace and glue it to the bottom of the pinafore. Tie a small bow and glue it to the neck.

8 Put a little bunch of dried flowers in the basket when you have finished decorating the figure.

pinafore

cloak   cloak

basket

bonnet

Huntsman

The Huntsman keeps watch in the forest so that girls like Little Red Riding Hood can walk safely without meeting the hungry wolf.

1 Make the basic figure as shown on pages 12–13.

2 Cut two jacket sections (see page 22) and position them so that they meet in the middle.

3 Indicate the buttons with a ballpoint pen.

4 Cut and position strips for the belt and strap and also for the cuffs and tops of the boots. Use a small sausage to make a buckle.

5 Cut two pockets from a sheet of dough (see page 20) and make a hunting bag in the same way. Position them as shown in the illustration.

6 Cut a scarf from a sheet of dough and arrange it around the neck.

7 Make a gun as shown in the illustration and position it under one arm. The barrel is made from a stick.

8 Mould a hat by pressing one ball of dough flat. Place another ball on top to form the crown.

9 Use a modelling tool to mark around the bottom edge of the trouser legs.

10 Make hair, the moustache and a beard with a garlic press.

11 When the figure is baked and decorated, glue a little plastic hunting horn next to the bag.

The wolf hiding in the bush (see the colour illustration on page 53) should be made with pointed ears and an open mouth with a long, lolling tongue. Place the head on a sheet of dough, covered with dough squeezed through a garlic press.

Grandmother

Grandmother is wearing a nightdress because she is ill, but she is happy because Little Red Riding Hood is on her way to visit her.

1 Make the basic figure as shown on page 14. Cut the nightdress so that it is long enough to reach down to the figure's feet.

2 Use a modelling tool to decorate the front of the nightdress and use a ballpoint pen to indicate the buttons.

3 Cut narrow strips for the cuffs. Ruffle them and put them above the hands.

4 Cut a slightly wider strip for the collar. Ruffle it to look like gathers and place it around the neck.

5 Cut a strip for the frill around the nightcap, ruffle it and place it over the hair. Press a ball into shape to make the crown of the nightcap.

6 Cut a pocket handkerchief from a sheet of dough, fold it loosely and put it in one of the hands.

7 Roll two small balls and attach them to the shoes, marking them with a toothpick to make them look like woollen pompons.

8 When you have baked and decorated the figure, make some spectacles from wire and glue the side pieces to the sides of the head. If you like, glue a small plastic glass into one hand.

ruffle the edge of the nightcap before attaching it

mark pompons with a toothpick

ruffle the collar before attaching it

Little Red Riding Hood (see page 50); the Huntsman and the wolf (see page 51); Grandmother (see page 52).

THE SWINEHERD [57]

The swineherd, who is really a poor prince, is seen surrounded by his pigs, and on page 56 is one of the ladies-in-waiting who served the princess, who threw away the nightingale and the rose.

1 Make the figure as shown on pages 12–13.
2 Cut two jacket sections from a sheet of dough and position them around the figure. Fold the edges outwards. Cut the collar from a sheet of dough and place it around the neck.
3 Cut a narrow strip and place it on the front of the trousers, using a ballpoint pen to indicate the buttons.
4 Cut the hat brim from a sheet of dough. Place this around the swineherd's head and fold it upwards. Mould the pointed crown from a ball of dough and place it above the brim.
5 If you wish, make a piglet (see page 55) and tuck it under one of the swineherd's arms.

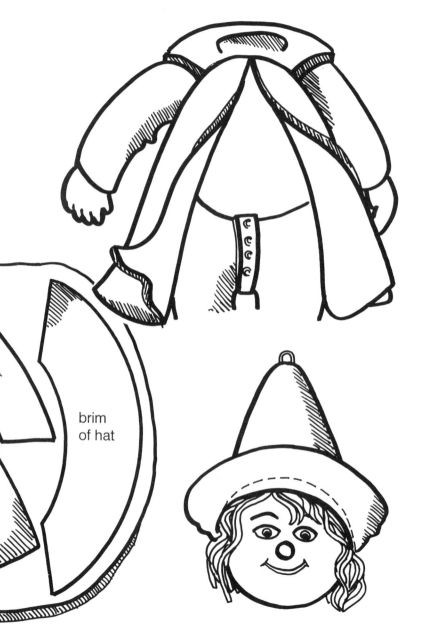

jacket

jacket

collar

brim
of hat

54

Pigs

The pigs are quick to make and you only have to paint the eyes.

1 Take an egg-shaped ball of dough for the body.
2 Roll a ball for the head and a smaller ball for the snout.
3 Press the snout flat and attach it to the head. Use a toothpick to mark the nostrils.
4 Attach the head to the body.
5 Roll four small sausages for the legs and press them into shape.
6 Use scissors to trim the trotters to shape.
7 Attach the legs to the body, smoothing the dough with water and a modelling tool so that the join cannot be seen.
8 Roll a thin sausage for the tail, attaching it so that it curls.
9 Mould two small ears and attach them to the head.

Lady-in-waiting

The fine lady-in-waiting has to take care not to get the mud and dirt from the pigsty on her dress.

1 Make the basic figure as shown on page 14.
2 Make the dress long enough to reach down to the feet and make it low-cut at the front.
3 Cut two round pieces for the overskirt from a sheet of dough and place them at the sides of the dress.
4 Decorate the overskirt by making two flounces from small circles of dough and pressing them to the hips. Make a bow for the centre of the skirt. Alternatively, make a belt and two small bows.
5 Make one or two small bows for the hair.
6 Make a nightingale as shown in the illustration below.

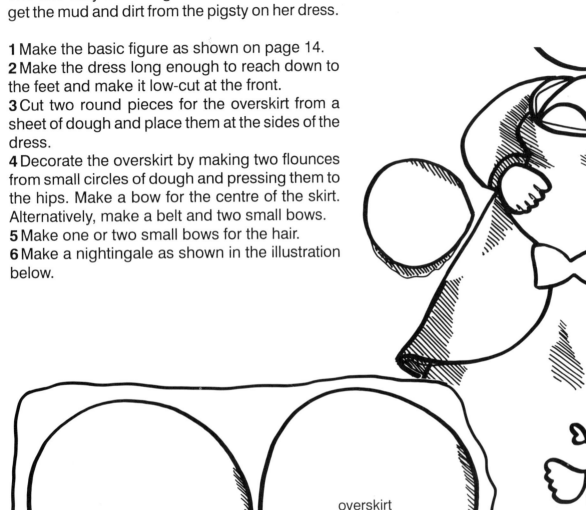

overskirt

overskirt

56

The swineherd (see page 54); the pigs (see page 55); ladies-in-waiting (see page 56).

WEE WILLIE WINKIE [61]

This is the perfect figure to place over a child's bed so that he can keep watch and make sure that the child is sleeping soundly.

1 Make the basic figure as shown on pages 12–14, but do not put trousers on. Instead, the figure wears a nightshirt that reaches below the knees.
2 Cut two narrow strips. Place one on the front of the nightshirt and indicate buttons with a pen.
3 Place the other strip around the neck to .
4 Roll a thick sausage for the bottle of sleeping dust and make a cone from kitchen foil and push it into the top of the sausage. Fold one arm around the bottle.

5 Cut a nightcap from a sheet of dough. Place it around the head and press the pointed end downwards.
6 Cut two umbrella sections from a sheet of dough. Roll a large ball and place it on one of the sections. Place the other section over it and press the two section together along the rounded edge.
7 Push one end of a stick up into the umbrella and the other end down into one hand so that Wee Willie Winkie looks as if he is holding the umbrella.
8 Finally, push a short piece of matchstick into the top of the umbrella to make a ferrule.

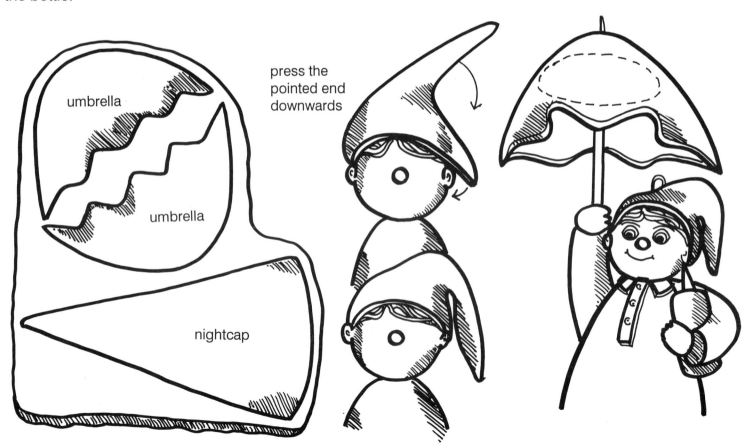

umbrella

umbrella

nightcap

press the pointed end downwards

HANS CLODHOPPER [61]

Hans Clodhopper rode on a billy-goat to woo the princess. He held a dead crow and an old wooden shoe and filled his pockets with sand.

1 Roll a large ball for the goat's body.
2 Make the basic figure as shown on pages 12–13, making the trousers reach down below the knees. Fit the legs around the goat's body.
3 Cut two waistcoat sections from a sheet of dough and place them on the figure.
4 Cut two triangles for the shirt collar and place them so that they lie over the waistcoat.
5 Roll a ball for the goat's head and press it into shape. Attach the head to the body.
6 Mould the ears and horns of the goat, using short pieces of wire to strength the horns. Attach the ears and horns.

7 Use a knife to cut the goat's mouth and roll a small ball for the nose. Attach the nose.
8 Roll four small sausages for the legs and attach them under the body. Use matchsticks to strengthen the legs so that they will not snap off.
9 Snip at the goat's body with the points of a pair of scissors to make it look like fur.
10 Make a beard and tail for the goat with a garlic press.
11 Use the colour illustration on page 61 as a guide to mould the crow and the wooden shoe and put them into Hans's hands.

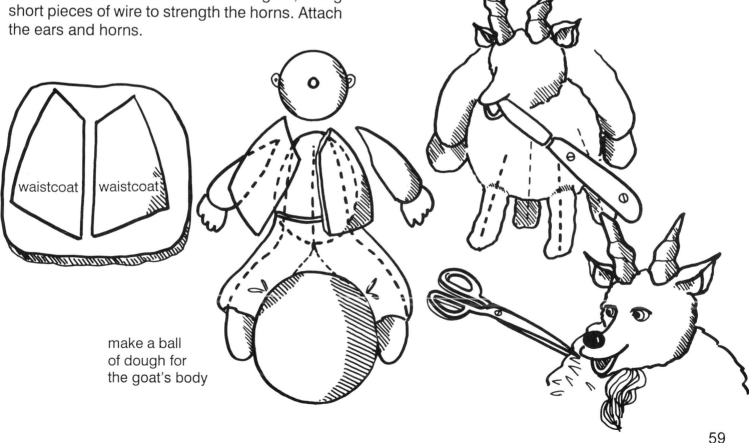

waistcoat waistcoat

make a ball
of dough for
the goat's body

THE WOMAN WITH THE EGGS [61]

The woman with the eggs is on her way to market with her big baskets full of eggs and the chickens around her feet.

1 Make the basic figure as shown on page 14. Cut the dress so that it reaches down to the feet. It should have an opening at the front.

2 Cut out a blouse as explained on pages 12–13 and fit the blouse and arms to the figure before putting the dress on.

3 Take two narrow strips from a sheet of dough and attach them to the arms to make the rolled-up sleeves.

4 Cut a wider strip and place it over the brow as an under-scarf.

5 Cut a triangle from a sheet of dough to make another scarf. Place it around the head and fold the excess dough behind the head. Tie the ends of the scarf below the scarf below the chin before attaching the head to the body.

6 Cut a circle from the sheet of dough. Before folding it to form the basket, use a real basket to impress a pattern on it.

7 Roll some small eggs and place them in the basket before balancing the basket on top of the head. If you prefer, put a piece of dough in the bottom of the basket so that you don't have to make so many eggs.

8 Press the arms into shape so that they are holding the sides of the basket.

9 Make two chickens as shown in the illustration below and attach them to the woman's feet.

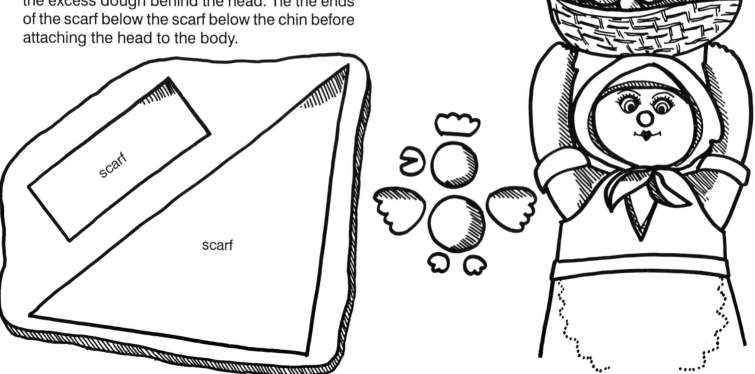

scarf

scarf

Wee Willie Winkie (see page 58); Hans Clodhopper (see page 59); the woman with the eggs (see page 60).

KING

The king is in full dress and is holding his sceptre and orb in front of him. He is illustrated on the front cover.

1 Make the basic figure as explained on pages 12–13. The trousers should reach below the knees.

2 Decorate the front of the trousers with a modelling tool and use a ballpoint pen to indicate the buttons.

3 Cut two waistcoat sections from a sheet of dough. Put the waistcoat sections in place and press them together in the centre.

4 Cut two narrow strips from a sheet of dough for the edging around the bottom of the trousers .

5 Model two buckles for the shoes.

6 Cut three slightly wider strips from a sheet of dough, fold them concertina-style and place them, one over the other, at the neck to make a jabot.

7 Cut two coat sections from a sheet of dough and put them in place.

8 Roll thick sausages for the fur edging up the left and front opening and around the cuffs. Mark the sausages with a comb to make them look like fur.

9 Make a sceptre and orb from wooden beads and matchsticks. Attach them to the hands.

10 Cut a crown from gold foil and attach it to the head. You could use the container for a night-light; use spray adhesive to colour it gold and make holes in it with punch pliers.

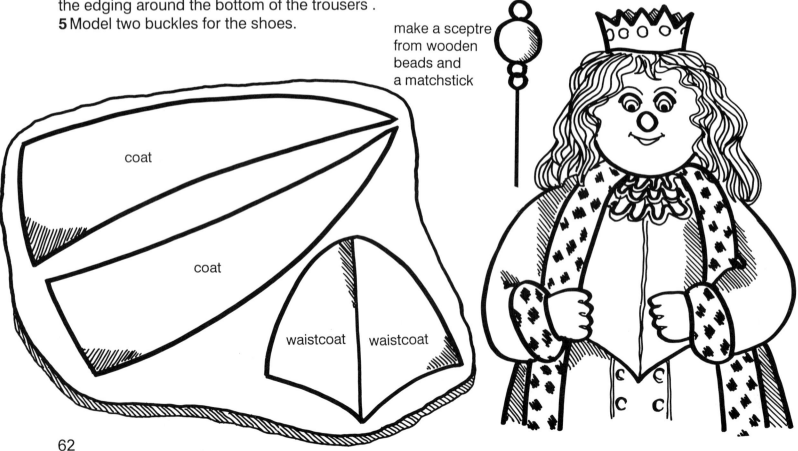

make a sceptre from wooden beads and a matchstick

coat

coat

waistcoat waistcoat

QUEEN

The queen goes everywhere with the king. She is always by his side in case he needs her. She is illustrated on the front cover.

1 Make the basic figure as shown on page 14. Cut the dress so that it reaches to the feet.
2 Cut overskirt pieces from a sheet of dough and put them in place, ruffling them slightly so that they fall in gentle folds over the dress.
3 Cut a belt from a sheet of dough and put it around the waist.
4 Model two small roses (see page 30) and place them on the overskirts (see colour illustration on front cover).

5 Cut two sleeve pieces from a sheet of dough and place them over the arms.
6 Fold a small, narrow piece of lace into a concertina and put it around the neck.
7 Roll small balls for the earrings and attach them.
10 Cut a crown from gold foil and attach it to the head. You could use the container for a night-light; use spray adhesive to colour it gold and make holes in it with punch pliers.

63

THE SHEPHERDESS AND CHIMNEY-SWEEP

The shepherdess and chimney-sweep are sitting on the chimney and gazing out over the night sky.

1 Roll a sheet of dough, about 10mm (½in) thick, and cut out the roof as shown.

2 Cut narrow strips for the tiles, decorating them with horizontal and cross-wise lines. Cut out the strips so that the edges are slightly crinkly.

3 Place the strips on the roof, beginning at the bottom, so that they overlap slightly.

4 Mould the figures, using the back view as a guide.

5 Model the legs of the chimney-sweep so he looks as if he is going down the chimney.

6 The shepherdess is made in the same way as the basic figure shown on page 14.

7 Cut the clothes from a sheet of dough, using the illustration as a guide.

8 Mould the chimney-sweep's hat from two pieces of dough and place it on his head.

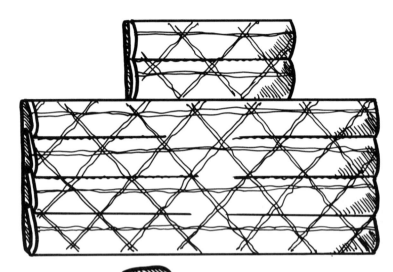

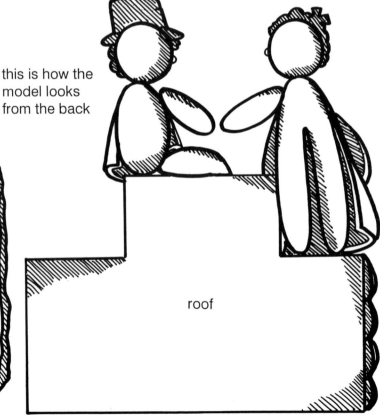

this is how the model looks from the back

roof

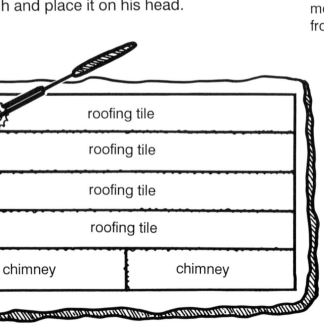

roofing tile

roofing tile

roofing tile

roofing tile

chimney | chimney

The Shepherdess and the Chimney-sweep (see page 64).

THUMBELINA

Thumbelina is very small, and she is sitting on a waterlily leaf and watching all the things that are going on in the water beneath her.

1 Cut a piece of wire mesh in the shape of a waterlily leaf, which will be used as an armature for the leaf. If you do not include this, the leaf will crumble during baking.

2 Roll a sheet of dough and cut two leaves, each slightly larger than the mesh.

3 Place the mesh leaf between the two dough leaves, and press the edges of the dough together so that the mesh is not visible. Bend up the sides of the leaves slightly all the way round.

4 Cut a cone from an egg box (see page 42).

5 Roll two small sausages for the legs and press them to the cone.

6 Make the dress, arms and head as described on page 40. Don't forget to use a matchstick to support the head. Cut a small bow from a sheet of dough and attach it to the hair.

7 Place Thumbelina in the centre of the leaf, decorating her as shown on the back cover.

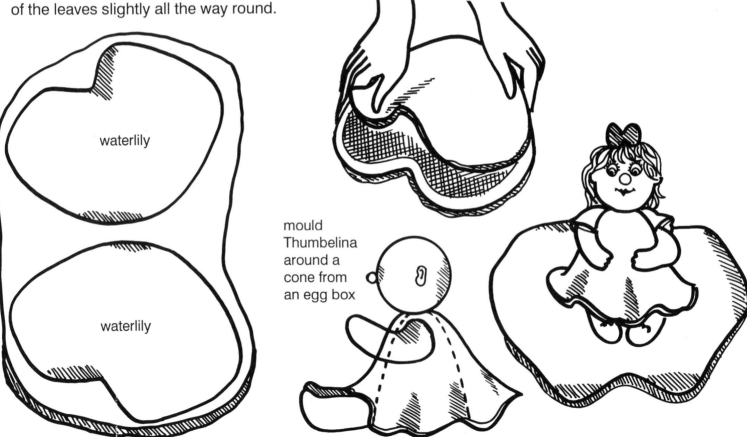

waterlily

waterlily

mould Thumbelina around a cone from an egg box

THE EMPEROR'S NEW CLOTHES [69]

The emperor has some new clothes, and he is out walking through the town so that everyone can admire them. But people are gaping in amazement – he isn't wearing anything.

Emperor

1 Make the basic figure as explained on pages 12–13.

2 Cut a nightshirt from a sheet of dough.

3 Cut a narrow strip from a sheet of dough and place it on the front of the nightshirt. Indicate the buttons with a ballpoint pen.

4 Mould two buckles for the shoes.

5 Make a sceptre out of wooden beads and a matchstick.

6 Cut a crown from a sheet of dough, mould it into shape and place it on the head.

mark buttons with a ballpoint pen

make a sceptre from wooden beads and a matchstick

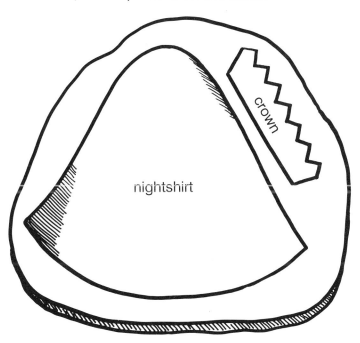

crown

nightshirt

Footmen

The footmen are carrying the canopy to protect the emperor from the wind and rain as he walks about town.

1 Make the basic figure as shown on pages 12–13. The trousers should be cut full so that they bag at the knees.
2 Mark the shirt with a modelling tool and indicate the buttons with a ballpoint pen.
3 Cut two sleeves from a sheet of dough. Put the sleeves in place so that they puff out slightly.
4 Cut narrow strips for the belt and strap and put them in place.
5 Mould the brim of the helmet by pressing a ball flat and mould the crown from another ball. Cut a narrow strip and lay it across the top of the helmet so that it runs from back to front.

6 Make a moustache with a garlic press and put it in place.
7 Place one of the arms around a carrying pole.
8 Roll a thick sausage for the canopy. Use a garlic press to make the fringe, and attach the fringe under the sausage. Cut a long, narrow strip from a sheet of dough and attach it where the fringe joins the top of the canopy.
9 Press the two carrying poles up into the canopy, but take care that they do not go through the top.
10 Make the two ornamental finials out of wooden beads and matchsticks. Glue the beads in place and push the matchsticks down into the dough.

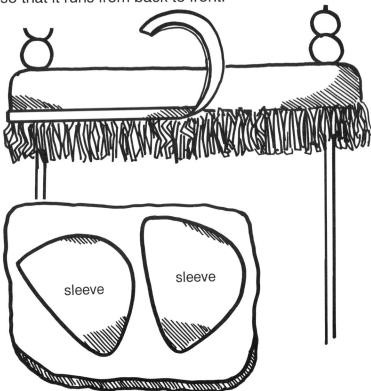

sleeve

sleeve

68

The Emperor's New Clothes (see pages 67–8).

THE STEADFAST TIN SOLDIER [76]

The brave tin soldier, who only had one leg, fell from a third-floor window and had lots of adventures, although the ballerina is always in his thoughts as he floated through the streets in his paper boat.

The Tin Soldier

1 Make the figure as shown on pages 12–13. Cut one of the legs off at the knee .

2 Mark the centre of the jacket.

3 Cut narrow strips from a sheet of dough to make the belt and strap, and put the pieces in position.

4 Make a belt buckle.

5 Cut narrower strips of dough to make the gold braid and put them in place.

6 Press six balls flat to make buttons for the jacket and put them in position.

7 Make epaulettes from two flattened balls of dough, mark them with a modelling tool and put them on the shoulders.

8 Roll the crown of the hat and cut a brim from a sheet of dough. Put the hat on the head.

9 Cut narrow strips from a sheet of dough for the strap and band of the hat. Press two balls flat and attach them to the sides of the hat.

10 Make a moustache with a garlic press.

11 When the figure has been baked and decorated, glue a feather to the front of the hat.

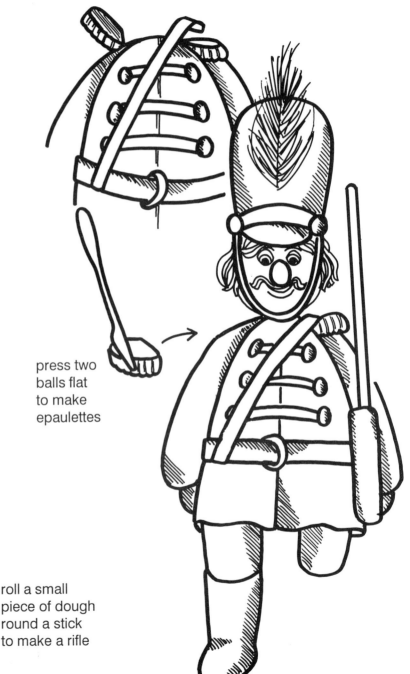

press two
balls flat
to make
epaulettes

roll a small
piece of dough
round a stick
to make a rifle

Ballerina

1 Make the basic figure as shown on page 14. One leg should point out to the side.

2 Cut the dress from a sheet of dough, making it very full, and place it around the body.

3 Cut two sleeve pieces from a sheet of dough and place them around the arms.

4 Mark the folds of the dress with a modelling tool.

5 Cut two collar sections from the sheet of dough and put them in position.

6 Cut narrow strips from the sheet of dough, fold them concertina fashion and place them around the legs to look like the frills of pantaloons.

7 Cut a cap from a sheet of dough, use a straw to make holes and place it on the hair.

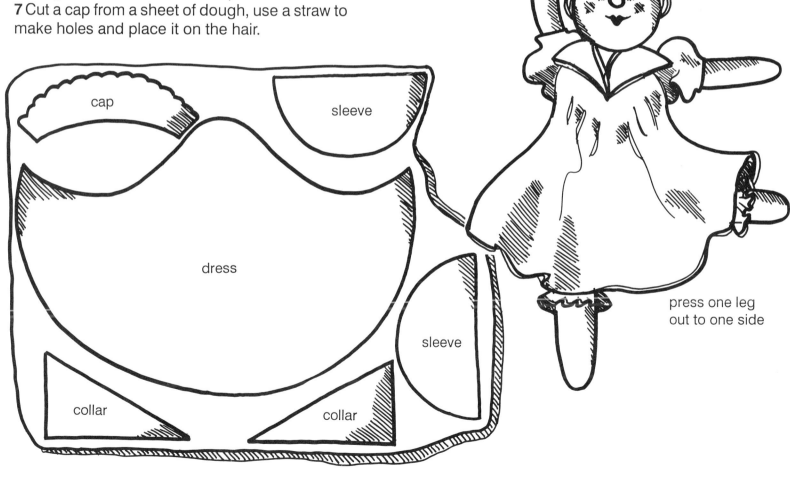

cap

sleeve

dress

sleeve

collar

collar

press one leg
out to one side

GOLDILOCKS AND THE THREE BEARS [73]

Goldilocks is sleeping happily in the bed with a fine lace quilt when the three bears come home.

Goldilocks

1 Roll two sausages for bedposts, one slightly longer than the other.

2 Cut the base of the bed from a sheet of dough. Attach the posts either side of the bed.

3 Roll a ball and press it flat to make a pillow. Place it next to the longer bedpost.

4 Roll a ball for the head and make the hair with the garlic press. Cut a small bow from a sheet of dough. Place the head on the pillow.

5 Roll a small sausage and place it on the bed. Cut a quilt from a sheet of dough and put it on the bed, over the sausage.

6 Place a narrow piece of lace over the quilt, cut a wider strip from a sheet of dough and place it over the edge of the lace.

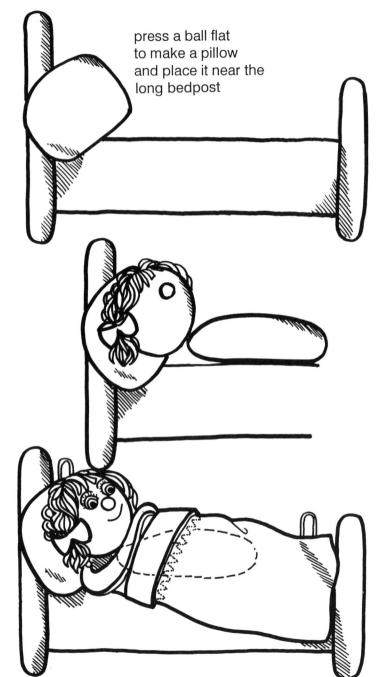

press a ball flat to make a pillow and place it near the long bedpost

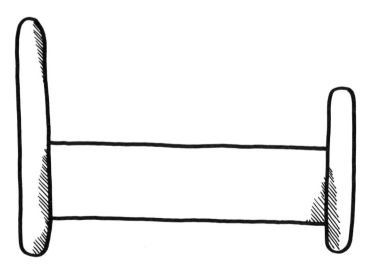

Goldilocks and the Three Bears (see pages 72–4).

The Three Bears

1 Make the basic figure in three different sizes as shown on pages 10–11. The figures should be slightly oblong.

2 Roll small balls for the noses and put them in place.

3 Roll small balls for the ears, press them flat and attach them to the heads.

4 Make the clothes as shown in the illustrations and put them in position.

waistcoat

waistcoat

collar

pinafore

74

WITCH [77]

The witch is out on her broomstick on Halloween. She has a little owl with her, but you could make a black cat if you preferred.

1 Roll two sausages and place them side by side.
2 Roll a somewhat thicker sausage and press it on top of the other two, as shown in the illustration. This sausage will help fill out the figure.
3 Cut a dress from a sheet of dough.
4 Cut some small patches and mark the edges with a modelling tool. Fit the patches on the dress and place the dress over the figure.
5 Roll a sausage for the arm and press a ball into the shape of a hand. Put the parts in place.
6 Attach a long stick behind the witch as her broomstick and arrange the arm to look as if she is holding the stick.
7 Roll a ball for the head and put it in place.

8 Mould an oblong nose, with a wart, and mark the eyes and mouth on the face.
9 Make the bristles of the broom and the hair with a garlic press and put them in position.
10 Press a ball flat to act as the brim of a hat. Mould the pointed section and attach it to the brim.
11 Shape an earring from wire and attach it to the ear.
12 Make a little bird to sit on the broomstick.
13 If you wish, you could make a headscarf for the witch as shown in the colour illustration on page 77.

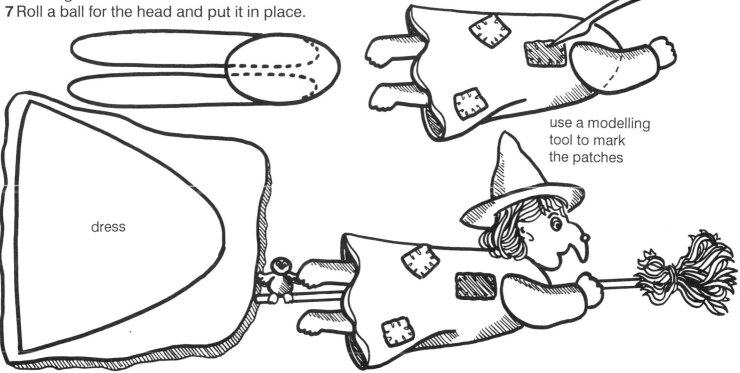

use a modelling tool to mark the patches

dress

The Steadfast Tin Soldier (see pages 70–1).

Witches (see page 75).